"The real power of these poems lies in the straight-talking appeal of the speaker's voice. Like a reliable engine, it powers the poems. When that voice interrupts description and intrudes directly on the narrative, the poems really soar. . . .The poems are sifting through the dark, the hard-bitten, in search of the glimmer of light that is transformative. That delivers magic."

—Mary Gannon, *Pittsburgh Post-Gazette*

"Daniels' gritty style and down-on-their-luck characters recall a line from Detroit rocker Bob Seger: "Beautiful loser. Never take it all, 'cause it's easier, faster when you fall."

—*Library Journal*

"Sometimes we need to read a certain kind of author because we simply have forgotten everything we knew about writing. We think we need a magic pellet, younger energy, more success, or to perform ritual—say like folding our hands and jumping off a building to get started. . . . Jim Daniels, we need you right now because we thought it was too hard to be natural while writing. . . . A real life is here. It lies behind the detail, but the detail is what we want. Jim Daniels' poems are human on the page, growing within and beyond some divine law of poetic order, far away from writers' disasters."

—Grace Cavalieri, poet and producer of "The Poet and the Poem from the Library of Congress."

In Line for the Exterminator

In Line for the
EXTERMINATOR

POEMS

JIM DANIELS

Wayne State University Press
Detroit

PS3554
.A 5635
I5
2007
0123539590

11 10 09 08 07   5 4 3 2 1

Library of Congress Cataloging-in-Publication Data

Daniels, Jim, 1956–
In line for the exterminator : poems / Jim Daniels.
p. cm. — (Great lakes books)
ISBN-13: 978-0-8143-3381-5 (pbk. : alk. paper)
ISBN-10: 0-8143-3381-8 (pbk. : alk. paper)
1. Detroit (Mich.)—Poetry. I. Title.
PS3554.A5635I5 2007
811'.54—dc22
2007016885

Publication of this book was made possible through the generosity of the
Ford R. Bryan Publication Fund.

Designed by Lisa Tremaine
Typeset by Maya Rhodes
Composed in De Generate, Trade Gothic, and Electra LH

CONTENTS

In Line for the Exterminator

a dark ride at Kennywood Park, Pittsburgh

Four skinheads swear and sweat
in fat leather behind my son and me
looping around endless rows of steel rails
in the fake cinderblock bunker. The ride
simulates a trip through the bowels of sewers
beneath the city. The skinny punks who cut in line
jokingly press the "panic button," a blaring echo
that mimics nightmare alarms. They won't stop
though somebody's shouting *stop it*. Some young blacks
with their girlfriends throw scowls at the skinheads.
Perfume and deodorant and farts and spit and melting
    make-up
and exposed skin pierced or not and tattoos and thick
    jewelry
and tight clothing plastered against skin of all colors.
My son is glassy-eyed with the room's menace—
it stings. It clings. The line crawls like a whipped dog
toward the dark door behind which it's promised
we are all to be scared. A fake newscaster on a monitor
describes a power failure. I want to ask "How many
in this room make minimum wage? How many
in this room will ever own a house?
What if we all made a giant wad of gum
and rolled it out of this park and onto the front lawn
of the richest motherfucker in this city?"

1

We have all paid our admission and had our hands
stamped. Perhaps the walls are
closing in on us. "Hey, how many of you
have been on this ride before?"

I. Last Picked

Last Picked

We slung mitts over handlebars and rode
onto pocked streets to look for a game.

Where does nostalgia end
and viciousness begin?

Sepia it up good. A slap
on the back for the good old

days, ditching each other, running
away when someone stops to tie

a shoe or take a pee, practicing
the ritual of betrayal so we'd be used

to it, like our parents. Where'd every-
body go? Cement streets never black-

topped over, never plowed, never patched.
They were what they were. And we too

were what we were. Nothing
to even scratch initials into

except our own skins. Where
does cruelty end and capitalism

begin? When do headlights
click off? When does the real work begin?

We selected a victim and piled on.
We called them nigger piles.

We were white. We made each other
cry till we no longer cried.

Till we just took it. Took it out
on every body that wasn't ours

or simply couldn't catch a lazy
fly ball, couldn't hit it out

of the infield. We scraped
scabs off each other's knees

till they scarred into protection.
Pick the kid with the new bat,

new ball, backyard pool. Spare
change. Pick on the kid

without. Pickers can't be
losers. Losers can't be

bruisers. We wore purple
and yellow skin. We hid

in each other's basements
and smoked tornadoes and drank

the warm piss of our fathers' beer.
Was it a *warning* or a *watch*?

We ignored sirens or we shouted
bring 'em on. We spit each other's

names, and the wind blew them back
in our faces and we smiled and called

each other friend, then kicked each other
in the balls. If you were driving past,

you didn't stop. If you were stopping,
you had no choice. The man who delivered

our mail hated us. He drank from his
leather satchel crouched behind hedges

by the grade school. He had nothing
for us. We were ready for the world

with our IOUs and postdated checks.
Cinders in our eyes, we winked at

bad TV and good radio and stomped
our feet and called it a dance.

If somebody lay beneath them
it was their own fault. Forgive me

Charles Fournier, David Lark, Eric Osinski,
Roy Cosmo, Terry Belcher, Timmy Trout.

Forgive me Audrey Spitza, Suzanne Bullock,
Barb Levitski, Lorraine Lipchock.

I've got a jackknife. A switchblade.
A stiletto. A prayer book tinted with red

sorrow, purple grief, Latin sins, and illustrated
denials. I've got dust and pebbles, swiped

change and cracked promises. The communion
of the sinners, the heavenly hosts, boasts.

Kick ass a compliment, not a threat.
I've already translated too much, the parchment

spontaneously combusting. I am turning
onto the old street looking for a game.

We're going to pick up sides.
We're going to see who's the odd man out

and finish him off like the birds we trapped in boxes
then tortured. Because we could.

Because no one turned down our street
to stop us.

Sugar, Sugar

We sat in Larry's icy scrap-wood clubhouse
listening to the year-end countdown on CKLW.
"Sugar, Sugar" by the Archies was Number 1.
Who would have believed that except Larry?
We'd kept betting him quarters till they moved
into the Top 10. He sang that song all day
bobbing his head like a Disney idiot, his smile
spreading over us like a cold we were almost happy
to have. We called him "The Brute" as a joke—
Larry never fought.

My brother garbage-picked that radio
over on Otis Street—or was it Bach?
I didn't know Bach, Johann Sebastian,
but I knew Otis Redding and how
he sang about love. We liked our R
with our B. We happily stumbled into
Dance Kings on the bare, frozen clubhouse
floor, eyes closed in dim light, swimming in
"The Land of 1000 Dances," imagining
Lynn or Anna or Cindy, waiting for the chance
to moan like that, like Wilson Pickett, like Marvin,
like Otis. We never criticized each other's dancing,
funky white chickens in heavy boots and coats,
our breath filling the air with moist heat.

We were dogs, humping the air
to CKLW, transistor batteries
fading in the cold, to Mitch Ryder, Aretha,
Bob Seger, our "Ramblin' Gamblin' Man."
CKLW's strong signal fought our parents
switching car radios to WJR's talky monotone.
CKLW—but even then, the Archies
were filtering in, a cartoon group.

Larry followed his ex-wife
to New York to be close to their daughter—
couldn't find work, went broke, came back.
His parents had changed the locks—
he stood in the street pleading with them
to let him in.

After the countdown, the Brute bought us burgers
at Oscar's with our own change. We laughed,
our boots dripping on the muddy floor
as we looked out toward Otis, toward Bach,
and the other streets we called home,
thought we could always call home.
We laughed and bobbed our heads, our bodies
burning under heavy winter coats, our voices
nothing like Bach, nothing like Otis, cracking
toward the future, where we'd learn
the world isn't sweet, sweet as sugar,
where we'd learn to dance, really dance,
and moan, really moan.

Balancing the Checkbook

My father's Dutch Masters box contained
a switchblade and a silver lighter
one antique condom and his corporal stripes
a wrinkled picture of his dead brother
a pen from Niagara Falls and the checkbook.

A dead mouse and simmering self-
loathing, a Not Good Enough pin
and a demerit slip, a night in jail
and the phone number of a dead Irish lawyer,
a scrap of paper scrawled Here's Where

Things Get Interesting. An empty lipstick tube
or a bullet. An empty church offering envelope,
an unintelligible hiss. One cigar. Five children,
but we wouldn't fit. Nights alone at the yellow
kitchen table flipping through the stack,

writing in the tiny lines, clicking
the pen against a longneck beer.
I'm three moons away, or hiding behind
the sliding kitchen door, listening to him breathe.
Everybody else asleep, and he's mine,

our planets aligned in the cold space
the moment the numbers add up

for one night, whatever's really
in that box shut away for another month
as he sighs *damn*—

the closest to *amen* we were ever
going to get.

Open House, Science Fair Project

I twisted a wire around a dry-cell battery
and a nail, then scraped the nail over a steel file

to make sparks. I was the nail, and the world
was the file. A simple story that proved nothing.

My theory was: fucked if you do, fucked
if you don't. That lump of a battery

sat heavy on the bare wooden table, already
draining, despite the appearance of density

and substance. The nail dangled from the wire,
waiting to be pounded in its next life

as was foretold by the seers of hardware.
The steel file would outlive us all.

My bad grade scrawled on a note card
wrinkled with sweat in my back pocket

where a wallet would soon be. And a comb.
Around me, other projects whirred and whistled.

My head lowered as if in prayer, I sent up spark
after spark, scraping my knuckles as I studied

greasy moons under my fingernails. Leaning on the
    table
were fathers who stood silent, and understood.

Self-portrait with Cigarette

I'm hunched into a streetlight saint
on the corner where Rome dead-
ends into Otis beside pricker bushes
planted to keep us from cutting off the angle,
though we've stomped them into ragged
bundles of thorns. Because twelve and counting.
Marlboro, my father's brand. Silver Zippo.
Numb fingers spark the wheel. Somebody scrapes
ice off a windshield, vicious jerking in the name of
    vision.
When the car finally passes, I emerge into my jacket,
brown corduroy, dirty fuzz at the collar.
Down the street, a muted yellow square
marks my house. Nothing ever breaks
the perfect glow.

Tonight I'm squinting through gray haze
into black-bearded snow—kiss, puff,
kiss, puff. Red glow fills the gap
between fingers. So I cannot cross them.
So I cannot flip you off. Cannot make
a fist. Knuckles cracked, raw. Because twelve
and counting, I fill my lungs with it.
I write my name with fire. I ash,
and it scurries over snow, disappears.
People with my last name will start

to die soon, but not yet. So I think
death's like that—the ash.
Because twelve. Because counting.

Slaughter Ball

We blasted each other, tried to
outlast each other, balls whumping
off bleachers, whizzing by teachers,
thudding off each other's heads.
Each time I said *I'm dead* it was
a finger-crossed prayer, an in-your-face
to God, a double dare. I palmed the dirty
white ball, that inflated world. My own
white face, a bloody kiss at thirty paces.
Simple enough then in dim high-school light
to believe that with enough muscle
we could survive unbroken. A nose
dripped rose on the warped wooden floor.
We laughed at the fallen petals.

Chocolate for Football

I dragged myself door to door, clunky
cardboard box banging off hip pads,
for CYO Football. Catholic football.
Catholic chocolate in long slender bars
wrapped in gold foil.

My own neighbors feigned a lack of recognition
if they answered at all. I watched TV through
their windows. October, Saturday afternoon,
college games on. Doors slammed,
smacked like shoulder pads.

*

On my bike after practice, I dragged my spikes
over cement in the dark, sparks flying up
and away like I was a Superdude or St. Fuckyouup.
Helmet hung over my handlebars, cheap logo
peeling off. Mouth guard glowing fluorescent
under spaced-out streetlights. Hoarse throat burning
as my soul escaped in a gob of phlegm.

*

They were replacing wooden bleachers
with aluminum. They were reminding us

we would live forever. We were asking
for support. We had plain chocolate

and chocolate with nuts. I was tired
of getting knocked on my ass by good
Catholic boys who played to win.
I was in love with the moon
and all reflected light.

*

At dusk, I lugged my box to the weedy hollow
in the empty field behind the bowling alley
where we stashed our sins—magazines
and wine. I ate till I was sick and left the rest
for rats and winos.

I wore one of the high strange numbers
of the uninspired. Three cheers
for Jesus, Mary, Joseph. Father, Son,
and Holy Ghost.

*

I paid for the chocolate with paper route
money. I egged the coach's house
on Devil's Night. I faked the need to go
and flattened the quarterback's bike tires.

My extremities were extremely
cold. I was blocking unsuccessfully

for the school's illiterate fancy dancers,
cheerleader idols, poster-boy martyrs.

Their saints were bigger than my saint.

*

When I quit the team, I kept the only things
that were mine: jockstrap, mouthguard, spikes.

If some night you were driving home from the Unimart
with milk, bread, a six-pack, a carton of smokes,

your cigarette lighter pressed in, waiting
for the orange halo glow,

and you saw a whirling miracle of sparks,
I hope you crossed yourself. Or smiled. Or swore.

Black Vinyl

A turntable circles in the dim light
of a damp basement. Apple wine swishes
cold and sweet down our young throats
while we float on black spinning,
volume cranked loud as we dare.

The Fish Cheer from Woodstock
spells the word we cannot speak
to adults, the basement word—
prayer and curse, praise
and passion, amen. Or the MC5:

On the 45, "Kick out the jams
brothers and sisters!"
On the album, *"motherfuckers!"*
We don't listen to 45s. We rarely speak,
staring away from each other
into black sound, thin layers of dust.

That stare makes our parents
cough. Our voices deepen overnight,
our hearts nearly scraped clean
of our parents' love, nothing new
to fill it with except more bass,
less treble.

At the end of the night
we wipe clean our thin discs
then sneak out drunk
to ditch the bottles.
Our hearts thump hollow.
Broken glass sings.

Cool

When Tom's dad died, wiped
out by a hit-and-run driver
between Toledo and Detroit
and Tom's face all cut up

from his cool sunglasses exploding,
I found out his dad's name was Arthur—
we'd drunk liquor from his bottles
till we grimaced and puked.

I clenched my teeth as Tom headed
down my street the morning after the accident
to walk with me to school—his mother
was a mess—he didn't know what else to do.

I met him at the curb, and we listened
to our steps scrape cement.
Passing the Mankewitz Funeral Home
we kept our heads down.

We stopped for a cigarette by the drug store,
like always, before crossing the street
to school. Somebody said something
about his face, like maybe a girl cut him.

Tom couldn't get any words out
of his dry swollen lips. I said
cut him a break, his dad just died
then we squinted out, away from him,

toward girls passing by, and hot cars,
and crossing guards, and teachers,
and parents heading toward work,
our living parents who didn't understand.

FM Radio, 1971

Jerry Rhodes handled his first AM/FM transistor radio
like a permanent erection or a translator
for his older brother's incoherent acid ramblings.
He constantly stroked the dial for a better signal
from WABX-99 while I stood awkwardly next to him
as if eventually I might get a turn. We smoked anything
that caught fire, listening to tinny versions of Jimi
and The Dead. We marveled at the calm demeanor
of the DJs. Jerry was going to be a veterinarian or an
    artist
or both. His long red hair matted easily, but he wouldn't
cut it. We'd been in Cub Scouts together and owned
    photos
of each other in faded blue hand-me-down uniforms
so we had to tell each other the truth. My brother
had disappeared on his motorcycle, resisting
arrest. Too cold to be standing outside like we were,
amid swirling snow in an empty field for better
    reception.
Our parents had leaned their disappointment
onto our thin, curved shoulders. We sagged beneath it.
The war wasn't going away, despite the shape of the
    table.
And when the wind was right, we could still smell
    smoke
from when Detroit had burned. Listening to Gil-Scott
    Heron's

"Whitey on the Moon," we understood that we were on
one moon. And black people were on another.
We would meet them some day, we thought.
We would give them the peace sign. Anything
was possible, given strong batteries.

Looking It Up

We found it in the library's fat dictionary
between *fuchsin* and *fucoid*.
Not only there,
                    but there
in the ways we used it, our fathers
used it: *bungled, usually used with up;*
to interfere, usually with "with";
to deal with in an aggressive, unjust,
or spiteful manner. Fucking:
Damned.
                It was good, fucking good
(*Very. Used as an intensive*)
to find it there, our monkey wrench
against soiled streets and sooty air
and jobs our fathers were saving for us
in their factories.
                    We're fucked,
we told each other, and laughed. And got
fucked *up* in the field behind school
passing joints, guzzling dark bottles,
clear bottles, so maybe we could sleep
through earth science knowing
all we needed: that cement
                            covered everything.
We took "Outdoor Chef," a course designed
for us, future shoprats. In the parking lot

we spelled it out in lighter fluid,
tossed on a match: *fuck*.
                              We gave each other
the finger and we fought, fucking each other
up on cement, asphalt, brick. Red lights circled
through our dreams.
                              We took "Drugs,
Delinquency, and Disorder," correcting
the teacher, the harried football coach.
We extorted answers in the required
government class, we fumbled
through speeches in the required speech class,
knowing all we'd need in those factories
was a good set of lungs
                              and the punctuation
of *fuck*. With its pimples, its greasy hair
and sneer, the word you couldn't turn
your back on—it drew blood, didn't fight
fair. The word we feared but never admitted
fearing. Like the name of an enemy—
if you said it enough times,
maybe it would go away, maybe it
wouldn't mean
                              anything.
We laughed and snickered
till the librarian shooed us away.
Sexual intercourse.
The first definition—we skipped over it
and never bothered to look up *love*:
2. An intense sexual desire
for another person.

                    I don't know
what to call what we did with girls
in backseats, basements, and weeds
except to say it didn't happen often,
the sad frantic couplings, jeans bunched
around our ankles, not at all like
we'd imagined, hoping for something
to curl up with inside that dark cave
lined with every time we said
Fuck.

Detroit, 1972

3:00 AM

At Top Hat Hamburgers
on the Detroit side of Eight Mile Road,
dirty snow smudging the curb
under glum streetlights, I gripped
the stainless steel counter
to keep the stool from swiveling.
The drinking age was eighteen. Or sixteen,
using the new math. I was exempt
from the draft and from playing piano.
Five years since the riots—under the new math,
yesterday. Outside, the world swirled past
in the stretched poisonous lights of every car
speeding through the sleeping world.
My first car slanted across the blurred
yellow lines in the lot. A black kid
maybe my age scraped the grill
behind the counter. Time scraped
the world off the dirty road, the clock
emptying out toward four, leaving
only the desperate, the lost, the over-
cooked. How did I end up there alone,
a blue sludge of blood above one eye,
sixteen, and flunking every quiz
on my future? The kid, maybe
my age, looked up at me. Oh,
we hated each other instantly.

Safety

Stopped at a red light near the freeway,
I opened a beer and threw the bottle cap
out the window where it hit pavement
and rolled. Where were we headed?
I closed my eyes. The light changed.
Hold my hand, she said. *I can't*, I said.
I'm driving. Some things you couldn't repeat
in a million years: it rolled right in the open door
of Olar's Last Stop Party Store
like a sperm shopping for an egg.
I opened my eyes. At sixteen, you have to wait
a long time for your head to clear.
Forever, sometimes. Later, we parked
and professed our love. Our hands were blind.
Would they ever get used to the dark?
How far would we go? We talked about it
like traveling when neither of us
had been out of state. The police stopped,
told us to keep moving. Stop, or keep
moving? Everybody telling us something
different. We tell more lies when we're sixteen,
and we ourselves believe half of them.
Like *I'll be careful* and *I love you forever*.
It was a miracle she never got pregnant
after all those long trips, crumpled maps
littering the backseat. I never told anyone
about the bottle cap. It was something to see.
Luck doesn't begin to explain it.

At Dinner, My Father Informs Us He's Been Laid Off

and we wolf down meatloaf and canned corn,
white bread and milk, racing to anchor
ourselves. *Stop slurping.* Five children, five
welts, five burrs. We grip the table,
my mother and father anchoring the ends,
my deaf grandmother floating away
on what she didn't hear, our leaky
lifeboat bobbing, shaking the Jell-O.
We all like red. *Lovelock and Piersall,*
my father said—his bosses at the plant—
and whatever came next bowed my mother's head.
I kicked the table. *Stop kicking the table.*
Lovelock and Piersall, and my father
was not hungry.
            Abbott and Costello.
Laurel and Hardy. Rowan and Martin.
Three Stooges.
            Three Stooges don't count—
three don't count. My grandmother hissed
at my baby sister, or maybe she was
passing gas. My father pushed away
from the table and started swimming.
We watched him disappear
hoping he'd be strong enough
to come back with help.

Elegy for the Sheik

The Sheik's pioneering sadism clearly established his credentials.
　　　　—The New York Times

In a tiny TV studio in Windsor, the Sheik
railed and raved. In our living room, we closed
the drapes to cut Saturday afternoon glare.
The camera withered under the Sheik's evil stare.
On the lumpy couch our father dozed
open-mouthed through our shouts and shrieks
and other comforting sounds of home: roof leak
and furnace groan. The Sheik's gory mumbled prose
translated from gibberish by the Weasel into a double
　　　dare
to Bobo Brazil or Bull Curry with the cauliflowered
　　　ears.
The *foreign object* ultimately emerged at the close,
stabbing a blood capsule open to please the studio freaks
and geeks. And us. Born in Detroit, Arab headgear
　　　notwithstanding,
the Sheik did not make cars. He made his landings.

Cyclone Fence, Detroit

Erected between yards to keep
each dog from having its day.
Muddy tracks along the fence line,

time's quiet rhythmic mess.
Life's Etch A Sketch moves
up and down and up, traversing

these streets where someone once
dreamt a trombone wail to penetrate
concrete, then died in his sleep.

Clock numbers shuffle
like a stacked deck of lottery cards
hypnotizing even unbelievers.

Tree roots revolt, raising sidewalk
squares into toppled dominoes.
In an underground bunker

the chosen are taught to scribble
their names beneath *sincerely*
as if it were a primitive ritual

one must endure despite
the lack of faith. Meanwhile
one dog sniffs and licks the fence

where another has pissed. Meanwhile
a driver closes his eyes and a car lurches
to a stop in bumper-to-bumper traffic.

He is driving to work. He is late.
Whose magnet pulls the cars through
the maze? Once a dog dug beneath

the fence and impaled itself.
Let that be a lesson to you all
was broadcast from a slow-

moving vehicle. The check
was cashed, and not another word
was moaned or howled or spoken.

Fossilized curses carved into cement
on the bridge to nowhere otherwise known
as The Overpass. We are constantly

underthrown. We constantly run back
to catch it. Once we went on strike. We waved
our orderly signs until they gave us

ten more cents an hour for the rest of our lives
or until the next round of layoffs.
Once we were fined for not licensing

our dog. In the center of the universe
we build cars. We are not unhappy.
Everyone remembers the two dogs

stuck fucking in the middle of the street.
We laughed till we choked,
till somebody got out a hose,

and we celebrated the miracle
of manufactured rain, indoor plumbing,
electricity, and fuel injection. The dogs

slunk away, collars jingling
like the soft bells of stars
we used to be able to see.

Petrified

My grandmother brought us genuine Indian vests
from Arizona. She arrived in Detroit broke
after a falling-out with her companion Hilda
and never traveled west of the Mississippi again.

She shared a room with my sister, a green plastic
screen between them. She brought us petrified wood
in tiny cardboard boxes labeled *petrafied wood*.
She and Hilda had gone west to keep house for a
       convent.

She drank a lot of tea, reading at the kitchen table
and in bed, as her vertebrae crumbled
into dusty pain. The green screen rattled like thunder
when she flung an arm out in her sleep.

Her four grandsons leaped across bunk beds
in the next room while she wrinkled the thin red
edges of her prayers. How does wood
become rock? How does your last good friend

betray you? We called her Little Grandma
as opposed to Big Grandma. If she minded,
we never knew. Her body hunched over its secrets
while we blossomed into sin. She'd wanted

to see the Holy Land before she died.
What happened in Arizona? Minerals
leeching in, leeching out. She became Littler.
The hollow ring of the telephone

was not for her. Hilda buried in a cardboard box.
The world a shell she held to her ear. Each night
we entered to kiss the shadow of her cheek.
We kept the petrified wood in cotton beds

in identical boxes. Jesus hung on crosses
in all of our rooms. Her rosary slept bedside
in a satin pouch. Hilda—a distant city erased
from her map to salvation. *Is she ever going*

to leave? my father asked under his breath,
though he knew the answer. Miracles
are real enough, if you don't define them
too strictly. The living turned to stone.

Death Seat

After my grandmother died, we fought
over who sat up front next to my mother
in the Ford Falcon with the metal dashboard
and magnetic Virgin and no radio.
My brothers and I had the hard heads
of holy youth, our brush cuts bristling
with electric eternal life.

None of us ever smashed our heads
into that glove box with no give
where my mother kept the old simple
hand-drawn maps to get my grandmother
to church and back, to the grocery store
and back. Bold black-markered street names,
and our phone number just in case.

My grandmother didn't buy a radio—she was already
going deaf. If the Virgin spoke to her,
she never told us. She shrank from crumbling
vertebrae until she couldn't see above the dash
and my mother took over at the wheel.

No one had died before my grandmother.
I know now there was luck in that—the oldest
being the first to go, following the map as directed.

We took turns being placed on the sacrificial altar
of the front seat, where we could easily die, lurching
forward into metal, where we could control
the imaginary radio, sliding the Virgin back
and forth across the dash to tune it in.

My mother drove that car for years —
she could afford no other.
She always knew whose turn it was.

Dreamscape

The sheer weight of my father's
pool table. Like a piano without
the lessons. He stroked the deep

green felt like intimate silk. He loved
to break, scattering the perfect vee.
Each morning he grimaced

a long coffee swallow, then disappeared
unarmed into the factory's oily cave.
He bought a short, weighted stick

for cramped corner shots. Soon enough
his four boys marred that perfect green
with reckless pokes and spills.

He invited neighbors for beers
and pool. We listened from half-
sleep to his loud pride.

He thought with enough chalk
he could make any shot.
My girlfriend and I knocked

balls together while we kissed
and groped. She sat on the edge
while I unzipped her jeans.

We were pool fanatics.
He bought a Ping-Pong table
to fit on top for family meals.

The factory slowly made him deaf.
The slate developed a pronounced sag,
and the felt eroded into baldness.

When he retired, he took
a chainsaw and cut it into pieces
to carry out the door.

No one remembered how
he got it down there.

Border Crossing

With random regularity, funeral processions
slipped down Ryan Road, past Eight Mile, crossing
from Detroit through Warren, my city—
Nine Mile Road, Ten Mile Road—
out to a black cemetery somewhere.
I knew not a soul who might be buried there.

Shiny cars full of somber black faces rarely looked
over at us as we stopped to stare from our ball field
near Ryan and Eight, our border community
on alert, inhaling suspicion among the weeds
on our crooked homemade diamond. Sneezing.

Ghost runners from the '67 riots
occupied empty bases, and right field
was an automatic out—we set weeds on fire
to try it ourselves.

*

Their long lines coasted through
our red lights that could not stop the dead.
I wondered why only black people died.
The earth was flat and went on forever.

Then Tony Bruno hit one all the way
onto Ryan Road. Darlene Sanders died
in a fire down the street, and we found out
where they buried white people.
Eddie Wakowski stole a bottle of whiskey
from a cabinet in Mankewitz's Funeral Home.

I joined altar boys, accompanying the priest
to the cemetery where he sprinkled holy water,
then slipped us each a few bucks in Mankewitz's limo.

I am riding in a long line of cars with little metal flags
and we are forever driving past factories
with their security cameras and guard posts
where our fathers disappeared. Where they
washed their hands at enormous cement
sinks, scrubbing off grease with perfumed sand,
drying their faces with rough dollar bills.

*

I worked at a liquor store on Ryan between Eight
and Nine. We sold pints to workers black and white.
Lunch-box sized. We cashed checks for whites only.
The earth was square. Nobody wanted
to fall off. Why not pretend to lose the ball in the weeds,
send the runner back to second, save a run?

A couple of weeks after we get robbed by two black guys
with guns who make us lick the cement floor and beg
for our lives, a car veers out of a funeral procession

into the tiny parking lot of Mestrovich's party store and
     out steps
a woman in immaculate dress and an enormous
     stunning hat.
She's yanking the arm of a tiny frightened girl. The
     wooden screen
smacks behind them as they rush in. The girl's gotta
go. Can she use our bathroom?

No customer ever uses our bathroom. White
or black. Girl's squirming. She's going to go somewhere
soon. Bruno Mestrovich closes his eyes and opens them,
his door swinging shut, then open. *Yes,* he says.
Go with the man, the woman says, though I am
a boy in all this. Though I have soiled myself
over a gun. The girl takes my hand, and I lead
her, wait, then
     escort her back
across the border. Outside, the procession is long gone.
But the woman knows the way.

The girl's wet hand squeezed mine.
I got paid in cash, a brown envelope labeled
with my name. Bruno died of leukemia six months
after selling the store to an Arab family. The world
is a sponge, and we are all drops of moisture.

This was after 1967, when Detroit burned and Warren
watered its own houses and we spoke in the clipped
     angry voice
of helicopters spilling soldiers onto the streets,

and processions of moving vans headed down Ryan
toward new distant suburbs. Weeds erupted out
of control. The cover came off the ball. Our bats
splintered, and we swore. A bowling alley landed
on our ball field, and we learned
to pay our money and bowl.

I loved Darlene Sanders like the eighth grader I was.
She had marked my neck with a kiss. I'd been bitten.
    Smitten.
The funerals continue to this day, down Ryan and out
to the distant wherever—I have still not been there.

I held my glove in my hand ready to catch anything.
I held the bat in my hand ready to swing away.
I had held a black girl's tiny hand. I spun the globe.

Abandoned, Detroit

We'd been waiting years for the old family house
of my father and grandparents and great grandparents
to fall, sneaking a quick daylight detour down
Benitau, slowing to look for the crumbling heap
of recognizable memory, then blowing through
stop signs back to the freeway.

Now, my father says *it's gone*. Anonymous rubble.
Dirt circling the lips of the monster everybody
has a name for. Though it don't come
when nobody calls. Don't look at me,
I'm not going anywhere. I take his word for it.

*

Last year, they moved out of *my* boyhood home
on Rome after 43 years to limbo-condo equatorial
     sprawl.
Nobody's driven past the Rome house yet.
O let me knock against that thick wood door
and have somebody let me in. Address and phone
     number
surgically imbedded like bullet fragments.

Laughing, clanging keys against the lock,
drunk against the silent house. I kissed that curb

10,000 times with my front tire. I shoved the truth
on scraps of paper through the sewer grate.
I nailed lies to the streetlight pole.

*

Okay, it's not true
that we rowed boats down the street
during the Great Flood. But we could have
if anyone'd had a boat.

The Flood—one of those American things, everybody
pitching in to clean up the sewage in each other's
    basements,
nobody talking about whose shit it was, and how they
were always the ones cleaning it up while somewhere
on higher ground the moon was laughing.

*

Ragged flakes of lead paint, yellow and brown,
seeping into the hallowed ground where our dead
were laid out, then carried across the street
to the church that is also no more. My heart's
a wrecking ball, okay? I'm swinging away
at my holy places of abandonment.
I'm thinking about bricks as seeds.
I'm dreaming the dull sad eye
of the streetlight.

Sandy Had the Kind of Laugh

you could hear across a busy street.
And I did the afternoon she slipped
into Gene's house, his parents at work.
She kept laughing and screeching *oh
stop*, then fell quiet. Later, she emerged
tucking in her shirt. I loved that laugh

but she had a crush on my older brother
who was wrestling the queen cheerleader
in our basement. Gene would have to do.
I was choking on cigarettes and cursing
my bike for not being a car. On the porch,
I sharpened a stick against concrete.

Ants swarmed over a piece of melted popsicle.
I squished them, gulping back tears. Time
sat on its ass while I squirmed and listened.
Lazy summer afternoons, she'd sat with me
there for hours, hoping for a glimpse
of the football star. She laughed at me

sagging in my muscle shirt. During a water-
balloon fight, I saw one of her breasts.
The day she laughed with Gene
my heart burst like one of those cheap
balloons. It'd be years before I made anyone
laugh like that, before I understood—

ants can't resist the sweetness. Pregnant,
senior year, she dropped out to marry another jock.
Once I waved to her—she was back visiting
her mother, the baby in her arms. I was still young
and pimply and skinny and sad. But it was not real
sadness, her eyes told me. And she called me

Jimmy, not Jim, to make sure I knew.
She held up her son's tiny hand,
waving goodbye.

II. Digger's Body Shop

Digger, The Short Days

Winter morning in a kitchen yellow
with old smoke: coffee cup lands clumsy
and sloshes, furnace kicks on, toast pops up.
Three small warm things to carry against the day.

Black outside except for the streetlight's
lonely gaze. The clock on the stove,
caked with grease, still works.
It tells you to rise, grab
your brown sack, and head out
to the car door's icy slam.
The foggy poison of your neighbor's car
seeps into the air while he waits
in his house for it to heat up.

You crank your heater full blast
though you know it won't get warm
any faster. You grab the scraper and scratch
the icy glass. Everything seems breakable
but nothing breaks. You drive off, headlights
dim with dirty slush. It's a day like any other
in Detroit, December. The short days.
Driveways shed their bodies to the ice and snow,
the street's deep winter ruts.

What do you think of, mornings like this?
The three lunches lined up behind yours
for your children just rising for school?
Your wife who made those lunches?
You think about how close you can park
to the factory gate before you make
your run for it.

Digger's Lawn Care

Driving through the rich suburbs,
you critique the perfect lawns—
plush, green, hedged, fertilized.
No crabgrass, dandelions, clover—
*none of the things that make a lawn
interesting,* you tell Loretta.

*Those guys push pencils all week,
they got energy to waste—or the bucks
to pay somebody. . . . Besides,* you add
with a wink, *I like spending my extra energy
on more important things.*

She frowns—you haven't touched her
in weeks.

*

In a broken lawn chair, your ass
slipping below the aluminum frame,
you hold a beer like a torch to guide
your neighbor Gus over.
He grabs a cold one.

How about those Tigers?
   They're losing.

You toss the radio into the bushes.
Gus raises his eyebrows, laughs.

Nice day. You both stare
at a young woman in tight shorts
walking past. *Yeah, nice.*
Gus sucks in his breath,
puts his beer between his legs.

You laugh, slap his back.
Ah, Gussy, what a day.
You kick over your empties.
Suddenly, hedge clippers *whoosh*
behind you. Your wife holds them
at neck level. *My day off, Loretta,*
for chrissakes. She snaps them shut,
yanks them open. You close
your eyes and feel the sweat.

Digger's Leak

Today you beat the dog,
thinking he'd pissed on the floor.
Your son overflowed the bathtub
and water leaked through the ceiling.
You hand the dog a biscuit in apology.

What are you doing, anyway,
taking a bath? you ask your son.
He's thirteen. *I haven't had a bath*
since I was five.

That's a lie, but who cares.
That sounded wrong, but who cares.
Nothing like a good shower.
He's pale and thin. You don't know
where to begin with him. You weren't
paying attention early on, and now
there's no opening. *Overflowing*
the tub—Jesus Christ.

I was cooling off, he says, in a voice
that breaks, breaks your heart.
90° all week, and your house with no air,
bad as the plant. Sweat drips off
your forehead as you mop. You study
the ceiling—it might buckle, come crashing

down. *Yeah. Well.* Your son stands still,
waiting for something.
Apologize to the dog, you say.
Go ahead, tell him you're sorry.

Digger Laid Off

Eight years since the last time.
Never thought
it'd happen again.

Seniority's hole—
the deeper you dug, the safer
you felt.

At the unemployment office
you shuffle in line with the rest,
shifting from foot

to foot, a wobbling bowling pin.
Angry, but at who, what?

As a kid, you waited
in line for football physicals.
Naked, nowhere to hide.

You can't pick your eyes up
off the floor. If they ask you,
you will cough.

Digger's Bad Reception

A fight at a high-school party
across the street spills
into your yard. You turn down
the TV and stare out the window:
your son is out there somewhere.
Your car antenna bends, breaks.
Somebody's face shoved onto your hood.

You steam the windows with stuttering
breath. In the kitchen, Loretta dials
911. *Hang up,* you tell her.

*

You wait up for your son.
He is not hurt. He mumbles thanks
for staying put during the fight.
You nod, then hurry off to bed.

*

In the morning, you examine
your car: hair and blood clotted
on the hood, antenna twisted
on the concrete. A bloody wad
of gum stuck to the windshield—
you knock it off, leave the rest.
It looks like rain.

Digger Gets a Checkup

The lab report says you have 15.2
years left. An extra .6
with an annual rectal.
.8 if you quit drinking.

You pop open another beer:
.8—*as if I ain't lost five already*.
You flip through a pile of bills,
the doctor's on top. You bump
the beer, and it spills off
the table's edge.

Your hand missing one finger,
the day the press surprised you.
You remember how that finger
used to point. How it knew
where to place the blame.

Digger Kills Time at the Clock Restaurant

Another cup of coffee
please. Regular.

An ulcer snuck in the door
ajar from another hangover.
Numb, you didn't notice
the breeze. Bored, it liked
your hospitality.

Now, it sends postcards
from exotic locales.
Wrong address, you reply.
Return to sender.

Coffee's on the *bad* list
but it's not as bad as other things
on the bad list. The hour is late
but not late enough.

You'll stay till the last-call club
has paid its dues, and the bars
have bolted their steel doors.

Some will come here to spread smoke
and boozy breath. Maybe you'll nod
and feel sad, or shake your head and smile
while your heart pounds its angry fist.

You're good for a drunkard's tip.
Another cup, yes—please.

Digger's Body Shop

Gear grind of something *wrong*
wrong wrong, your mother's voice
on the phone wanting someone to come
pick her up please off the floor.

You swipe your napkin
over your chin. *Guzzle your milk,*
son, we gotta drive over and pick
up grandma, she fell again.
Off you go in your Mercury. Kid
wants to drive, but you won't let him.

The old days, you had your basics:
change air filter, oil, oil filter,
new plugs, points, water in the battery.
Radiator flush and fill. All the boy can do
is read a dipstick. Maybe that's all he needs.

Lying under a car, dark grease and solid metal.
Calm as a surgeon with all the time in the world.
You oughta try it sometime, just hanging out
under a car.
    Dad, don't get weird on me,
    Grandma's gonna be okay. Right?

Positive to Positive, Negative to ground.
Acid turns a rag to confetti from hell.
Nostalgia for the magic smell of Go-Jo.

Guitar screech and wail—
Hendrix, he's my man.
    Dad, watch the road.
Glad I got her that portable phone.

No broken hip this time. *Go finish*
your dinner, she says, comfortable
in her chair again. You wipe her chin
with a stained hanky. *Little jam there, Ma.*

Shoot me when it's time, son, you say
calmly. He smacks you hard in the shoulder.
You crank it louder. He says nothing.

Digger Gives Away the Bride

Shaving in the mirror, blood seeping
into your white collar, skin scraped
raw, and *we're late, hurry, we're late.*

They can't start without me, you shout,
pressing a towel against red blotches.
She's nineteen, damn it, you say
one more time. At the church,
it's got to be all smiles.

And I was nineteen too, she says
one more time. You wonder
if she's taunting you. *And you still
love* me, *right?*

Of course, you say. Today's not the day
to split hairs, call names, or grimace
in public. *Yeah, but he's an asshole,*
you whine helplessly.

So are you, dear, she says, and you laugh.
Next thing it'll be grandkids,
and retirement, and what? *I'm ready
to limbo,* you say, and put on your jacket.

How low can you go? Your daughter's
dressing at church with her friends.
Your shoulders sag in the crisp jacket
as you step outside and look up

into clear blue, impossibly blue skies.
Two vapor trails criss-cross.
Can't we stay home and just enjoy this?
No answer for that. *And what?*

Not even a cigarette to help you
through. You've been doing
the retirement math. Nobody's
going to miss you at the plant.

They *can* start without you. *These shoes.*
Man, I can already feel the blisters.
Your own wedding, last time you wore a tux.
Loretta looks like a Lawrence Welk

reject in her flouncy dress. And you're
the drunken emcee at the fixed beauty pageant.
But there's no denying the sky. *And what?*
How low can you go? How high?

She's in the car waiting for you with a smile
that'll take you to heaven one second
at a time. Your finger traces one vapor trail
as it moves across the sky, rounds back
toward a perfect circle.

Digger Watches the Neighbors Move Out

to a bigger home in a distant suburb
gobbling up the old farms your father
used to drive past, just to show you
a way to get lost.

                 Just when their kids
are moving out, they go and buy
something *bigger*? For Sale signs
litter four lawns on your street.
No one mentions the blacks who moved in
on the next block—their lawn greener
than yours ever was or will be.

                      You'd dreamed
the boxes on your street would always be filled
with the same reliable gifts. The Poluskis'
grandson turned their place into a refueling stop
for random drunks. The Wanieckis' kids fought
over the meager inheritance of their parents' home
until weeds choked it, until the house said *I give*
and was sold for a pittance. You put siding up
and got new windows. Staring onto the pocked streets
where your children scabbed their knees and laughed
and screamed, you press your nose to the glass
and watch the Kupchaks' kids pack the moving van.

Farmland. Low rolling hills. Corn rising
like happy kids lifting their arms
to be accounted for. Your children urge you
to join the exodus, be closer to them.
Safer. As if suddenly their own memories
are not good enough.
                        Night, and the van is gone.
On the porch, your emergency cigarette glows
like a stunned autumn firefly—tired,
easy to catch.

Digger Swallows the Worm

An accident in the plant, a hi-lo driver
casually turning a corner
swerved to avoid a ranting foreman
and dumped his load of axle housings
onto an unsuspecting mechanic tinkering
with a broken press conveyor.

Deuces Wild after shift change, a sullen
bunch pounding shots, ignoring chips
and pretzels. *An accident,*
you tell Loretta over the phone. *I'm okay,*
but I'll be a little late tonight.

His name was T. J. You don't know
his full name. You helped pull
the steel off of him. Under the pile,
silence. The EMTs moved him so slowly,
your own bones seemed to break in the process.
The foreman got everybody working again,
except the hi-lo driver, Gnatkowski,

taken away for testing—another casualty,
his blood laced with liquor and speed.
Deuces Wild, formerly The Ritz,
formerly Bob's Pump House.
How long till retirement?

Each shot of tequila greases your grimace.
The hand of God vs. the hand of Gnatkowski.
12 rounds. T. J., a family man
with a speedboat he never used,
a dog whose name he changed.

You skip a couple of rounds
while the young bucks drink on,
invincible in their ignorance.
Just save the worm for me,
you tell them. When it is time,
you'll swallow.

Digger Loses His First Tooth

It breaks off
in the homemade peanut brittle
your old neighbor makes every Christmas.
This year, impossibly hard and thick.
She's losing it, you venture to Loretta,
poking at the black hole in your smile.
Who isn't? she asks. *Me,
me, I'm not losing it*, you shout.
In the mirror, a gap-toothed derelict
stares back, the one who betrayed you.
*Maybe the tooth fairy will leave you
something*, she kids. You wince at the cost
of a crown. *Fuck the tooth fairy*, you say,
your finger in your mouth
so it sounds like *ruff the oof fa-wee.*
In bed, you cover your head with a pillow
to cushion the blows.

Digger's Donnybrook, Senior Softball

You slid into him hard and gave him a shove.
Sixty-four years old and having trouble
sleeping, waiting for retirement.
He shoved back. Two old men falling
against each other, the young umpire not sure
whether to laugh or break it up, but the teams
swarm around you just like on TV,
so he has to intervene, the young hero,
wade through the quicksand of old men
with their well-oiled gloves. On the bottom
of the pile, a sharp pain pierces your chest.
It's a cracked rib, not the heart.
Not the heart, though each breath sears
with pain as the umpire makes you shake hands
like two squabbling kids.
It felt good to give him a shove.
Can't remember the last time you shoved
another man. The little guy shakes your hand.
His is trembling. In your sixties,
playing softball again. Not the heart.
You laugh, and it hurts.

Digger Turns in His ID

While thousands pass in two schools at shift change,
you are an old gray fish flailing between them,
trying to decide whether to be late or not
on your final day.

It's not like anybody can ease up on you:
a body always needed at your machine,
everything timed. Tomorrow, not even
your ghost will stand here. Another person
will don clean gloves, and soil them.

You scratch your name into your machine,
through the grease, through the pale green paint,
with your car key. Loretta packed Twinkies
in your lunch. And a note, says she loves you.
Twinkies—so soft—so hard to swallow, today.
What do I do with this? you ask, holding up
the note for your buddies to see.

*Wait till she's stuck with you home all day,
she'll be singing a different tune,* one guy says.
Your plan is only to buy a rowboat
with a small motor, putt-putt out
to a quiet lake and fish.
Water lapping against aluminum.

The clock's not going to surprise you
this late in the game—the hours pass
with stern efficiency. The plant so big
that outside your department, nobody knows
you're on your way out today. Today!

Foreman shakes your hand. Young guy—
ten years in. And the guys line up
and clink their lunch buckets against yours,
the factory high five, metal on metal.
God bless you, Spooner says. *Now,
don't go bringing God into it
after all these years*, you smile.

You want to keep your ID as a keepsake—
your life on a small laminated card—
but they take it. *Company procedure.*
Your pension will be good. You'll be *set*
for life. A lifer released—but not
for good behavior. Another body
used up? *Nah.* Drinks at the bar
tonight? *Just one.*

And what? Let's stop here,
while everyone's still sincere
and the map is empty once more.
Empty, but not disintegrating.

Turn the key in the lock.
That's right. Climb in.
Deep breath,
and start 'er up.

Digger's Property Assessment

You live in Warren, the third largest city
in Michigan—or the fourth. All you know
is the precise, endless weave of taut symmetrical
lines, and how you leave off *street* or *road*
or *avenue* or *boulevard*—just *Rome* or *Otis*,
Eight Mile or *Nine Mile*. Where you work—
just *Chrysler's*, *Ford's*, or *GM*.

Lawns squared out like green
American cheese, with the rigid edges
of crisp dollar bills before the handling,
the soiling. Your children gone,
the porch unpainted, the city saying
your house is worth less than ever.
Your dog still bites, but they don't figure

that in. They count on your rusty cyclone fence.
They don't figure in historical events:
your oldest daughter showing
her breasts once at dusk in August—
was it the heat?—a tattoo she lived with, then shed,
moving away, away, to where streets bend and curve
and cross each other, where hills offer their own

surprises. What else? Two men lived together
once. You laughed and winked. Until they kissed

each other hard on the street. Your best friend
Cletus retired and promptly fell asleep forever
in his attached garage. Attached garage.
Attached, you're attached, and cannot
move, despite the cell-phone static from the kids.

Your kids having kids. You're *Grandpa*
with your boring stories of the plant—greasy
blur of thirty-five years, the daily drive
from Eight Mile to Eighteen. Your wife Loretta
tuned instead to TV stories manufactured like cars.
Her friend Mavis next door got lost
walking around the block last month.

Impossible to get lost, impossible
to *not* get lost on your identical
streets. Did they take the whole
neighborhood and knock a few grand
off every house? Or did someone
peek in the smudgeless windows
and take notes?

Easy to get lost, kiss somebody
else's wife, pay somebody else's
bills, say somebody else's prayers
in somebody else's church,
repeating your lines in the longest
running show in history:
who dunnit?

You open Christmas cards
with the sigh of the bored bureaucrat
knocking you down another thousand,
with the sigh of your kids' old teachers
fondling vegetables in the supermarket,
with the sigh of the shrinking houses
with their expanding TVs.

How much is it worth to drive for miles,
walk in a house, and find the bathroom
blindfolded? And you almost need to
now—prostate trouble and beer nostalgia.
It takes all morning to open the mail
and think about writing the check,
filling in the boxes.

Walking down the street to the mailbox
that hasn't moved in fifty years,
you see a woman in her house
sit and lift the cover of a piano.
She breathes deeply and flutters her hands
in the air, playing silent notes.

Through the curtains, you watch
the puffed globe of her thin white hair
glowing like blue grace. She turns
to catch you staring, covers
herself as if she were naked,
caught. Yes, she's the one
you kissed and will not tell.

How much has that been worth?
Is it gaining or losing interest?
Somebody's grandson playing catch
with himself loses his ball beneath
a car. He crawls into darkness
and reaches, stretches. You can't
help him anymore.

You drop the envelope in the squeaky
slot, trying to remember the old
mailman's name. Your kids
would remember. Balls travel far
in Warren, Michigan.
If you get a good roll.
If you keep it on the ground.

III. The Shelter of My Father's Coat

Can't Sleep

Two days after Eminem (Marshall Mathers) abruptly canceled his
European tour, citing exhaustion and unspecified "other medical
issues," his spokesperson revealed that the rapper had been
hospitalized for a sleep-medication dependency. In response to
news of Eminem's hospitalization, a radio station was collecting fan
signatures on a twenty-foot-long "Get Well" card in Warren, Michigan.
Warren is in Macomb County, the area where Eminem grew up.

Marshall Mathers and I cannot sleep
tonight. We lie in bed and remember Warren,
the same city of our separate youths, the perfect grid
from Eight Mile Road to Fourteen Mile Road.
From Dequindre to Hayes. He is thirty-two.
I am forty-nine. He is the illegitimate son of my
    memory.
I count the blocks, I list street names:
Dallas, Otis, Rome, Pearl, Jarvis, Garrick,
Michael, Toepfer. Then, the families
who lived in every house, and the children,
and which factory the fathers worked in,
who dropped out of high school,
and who graduated. The names of the trailer
parks and places I got my ass kicked.
Where who got shot and who did the shooting.
Who got pregnant, who kept the baby. Who
didn't. But it's just six square miles,
and still I cannot sleep. If you drive
these streets, you might suddenly
and unknowingly end up in Sterling Heights

or Hazel Park, or, even Center Line,
but me and Marshall would know,
wouldn't we, Marshall? What are you
taking to get you out of the sleepless box
of Warren? I've got three bottles
in my medicine cabinet. Your mother could
have been any number of my classmates:
Lynn, Robin, Patty, Cindy M., Cindy R.,
Judy, Carrie, Marcy, Jill, Karen. I already
took one pill, but I think I need half
of another one. Our neighbor is silent
tonight, though last night he was pounding
a sledgehammer at 4:00 AM so hard it shook
our house. We didn't try to stop him.
His phone is disconnected. Etc.
It's that etc. that we have in common.
Me and him—and you, Marshall.
He's alone next door now. His two children
from two wives ago rarely visit.
Here, my wife and two children,
we stay put. Tonight offers no sledge-
hammer of an excuse. If only the houses
had an upstairs. If only someone had thought
to create a downtown. If only the GM/Ford/Chrysler
plant had not closed down or laid off half
its workers. If only someone one time
had been less cruel. Had gotten off us, let us up
before blood was shed. I used to crave
drugs that kept me up: speed, coke.
The jerky knife blades and shrieking volume
of rage. Tonight, the relentless silence

of the sledgehammer. The legalized
dancing monkey. Tonight it's Warren
on the brain, the dangling muffler
of what we thought we left behind.
Bullets in the bottles calling our names.

American Cheese

At department parties, I eat cheeses
my parents never heard of—gooey
pale cheeses speaking garbled tongues.
I have acquired a taste, yes, and that's
okay, I tell myself. I grew up in a house
shaded by the factory's clank and clamor.
A house built like a square of sixty-four
American Singles, the ones my mother made lunches
with—for the hungry man who disappeared
into that factory, and five hungry kids.
American Singles. Yellow mustard. Day-old
Wonder Bread. Not even Swiss, with its mysterious
holes. We were sparrows and starlings
still learning how the blue jay stole our eggs,
our nest eggs. Sixty-four Singles wrapped in wax—
dig your nails in to separate them.

When I come home, I crave—more than any home
cooking—those thin slices in the fridge. I fold
one in half, drop it in my mouth. My mother
can't understand. Doesn't remember me
being a cheese eater, plain like that.

Hot Dog Variations

I stuck potato sticks into my bun
and called it a porky pine. They
scraped my palette into bleeding.

My mother wrapped dogs in bacon
slit the side for a sliver
of pickle and called them gourmet.

A 2-for-1 coupon from 7-11.
They circled black on a spit under a pale bulb
and came back up on the swings in the park.

3:00 AM and we wanted to have sex again.
Downstairs, I boiled the dogs. We wrapped
them in white bread. We nearly choked.

I ate them cold from the package
rehearsing my speech about purity
on long-distance drug deliveries for Mad Mike.

God save the Hot Dog. Its wobble,
its cushioned fall into the bun. God bless
American condiments and baked beans.

It fell in the dirt, but I wiped it on my jeans.
It fell in the coals, but I wiped it on my jeans.
It fell off the platter, and I fought the dog for it.

I fought the dog, and the dog won.
Relish and love. Madness and mustard.
Don't choke. Don't wince when you bite

into something hard.
Grind it up and don't grumble,
don't mumble.

Lord, it comes spilling out the side,
chili and onions and regret.
Wipe the corner of your mouth.

Grin like a good American. Grin
and don't hit anyone. Grin and load up
the grill. Grin and click the tongs

like a hungry gator. Cheap paper plates
sticking together like pure love.
Eat with your hands, in a hurry,

eat when you're poor, when
you don't give a shit—
you just want to gulp it down,
get back to it.

Pastime Lanes Lounge

Friday night, my divorced brother trying out
his new girlfriend on us, the oldies funk band
so loud all we can do is dance and wait for a break—
she sways, arms tight to her chest, fists shaking
imaginary maracas. My brother's steps
have not changed—some vague c & w hip twitch
from wife #1. My wife and I do our usual spins—
she shrugs to the beat through smoke and twang.
Bottles slam wood, Detroit's rough elbows stuck out
like the stubs of wings—flightless birds, even on
Fridays, under the low ceiling.

We're a little gray for the Pastime—
but my brother wants a reality check
or an approval check or a blank check
to get on, get on, get on with his life,
get over his do-si-do and hard likker,
the hollow body of his old life.
She's shaking those maracas and bobbing
her head. My brother awkwardly places
a hand on her shoulder and bends
to shout in her ear. She mouths *what?*
He tries again. She shrugs. Someone
has taken our seats. We could be dancing
forever. I love my wife like he loved
his. Let's never get divorced, I'd tell her

if she could hear me—she wants to be here
least of all. The guitarist splashes in a muddle
of feedback, and they're off on break, sudden
silence crowding in. In line at the john,
my brother asks *what do you think?*
I'm not ready, I tell him vaguely, but it's good
enough for him. Past Time—my ears ring
and burn with it. Somewhere behind us,
balls drop and roll toward the pins.

Hooked

Frank, just out of rehab, pounds on his grandma's door,
but she's wise to him and calls the cops.

Her first grandchild—his mother, seventeen
when she had him. Last we heard, she'd kidnapped

some purebred dogs and was hiding out in a *borrowed*
van. The cops know Frank. They escort him away

with a warning. Shame doesn't work with Frank.
He wouldn't know shame if it smacked him upside

the head. Grandma's a pain in the ass these days,
but she doesn't deserve this. Grandma's hooked herself

on nerve pills. She pops them just to watch
her soap opera when something bad's happening,

and that's pretty much every day. Frank's daddy
believes in horse shit and bribes. He won't speak

to Frank—his latest theory is Frank wasn't his
to start with, though they look like brothers.

Since Grandma's was a bust, he'll probably break
in somewhere, though the police just stuck him

at the top of their list. Last time I saw Cousin Frank
was Christmas Eve two years ago—he showed up

with a woman, and a child he claimed was his,
though it turned out the math wasn't even close.

The baby was sick. Frank held it at arm's length,
looking everywhere but at the child, his extended

family looking to see what kind of story
he'd tell next. He probably just wanted

to be like us—borrow a family
for the holidays. Aunt Renee got

Grandma a glass of water for her pill
while Frank spoke vaguely of finding a job.

He asked no one for money,
and that was his gift.

92° today, and hotter tomorrow. Birds chirping.
Happy. Not much happens in the life of a bird.

Every spring I scrape a couple dead ones off my
    driveway,
fallen out of a nest in the eaves. If he hurts Grandma,

it'll be everybody's fault. We can't even find him tonight,
damn it. Me and Uncle Beano and Cousin Rudy and
    my dad

circling the streets, targeting his old haunts. And what
are we going do if we do find him? It's getting late.

We've stopped talking. Soon we'll give up,
head home to lay in bed, sweating our losses.

Tomorrow may bring a new episode, or it might be
    weeks.
If he's lucky, the police'll find him first, Cousin Rudy says

with forced bravado, punching his tender fist for
    emphasis.
No air in Uncle Beano's car. Windows rolled down,

our heads leaning out into it. *Sweet Jesus,*
my dad says, to nobody about nothing.

Driving Past the County Jail

erected between the Monongahela River
and the elevated Boulevard of the Allies
like a utilitarian apartment building for singles
or a retirement home for pensioned steelworkers
or the corporate headquarters of a company
specializing in adult novelties or a hospital
for veterans of domestic wars or a dormitory
for Duquesne University rising on the bluff
above it. But if it were any of those things
a woman would not be lifting her shirt
for her boyfriend at the barred window
and for every other prisoner and for every
car passing on the way someplace. Her breasts
bounce as she leaps up and down
as if she's not high enough for him to see,
as she shouts, *I love you, baby*, knowing
he can't hear.

Herbs and Blood

I grow herbs in pots in my cement yard.
I patch cracks religiously. Annually.
Futilely, like prayer.

A random *they* beat and robbed you
on your random street two blocks away.
Some believe prayer breeds forgiveness

through calm repetition. Blood
can steal your return address
and stain your clay pots.

I grow herbs for the strength
of their smells. Repetition promotes
healing. They penetrate like blood

spilled into memory. Your head against
cement. Sage = wisdom. Rosemary = heartbreak.
Lavender = comfort. Basil = uncertainty.

Oregano = complication. Impossible to steal
odors. Isn't it? My chair scrapes cement,
wedges in a crack. *Left for dead.* I dream

of sunflower heads eager on their stalks
to let things be. I make a note to spray the wasps
in the eaves. I never drive by that spot,

as though it no longer exists in this city.
You write slow letters from a place less humid
with tears. Desire contained in the rich soil

of these clay pots. Rubbed between my hands,
herbs spark and sparkle, fill me with shades of green
and a gentle hand, yours, reaching up. Survival

is one breath, then the next. Sage = superstition.
Rosemary = faith. Lavender = deception. Basil =
orgasm. Oregano = protection. Each dream

a luxury of mythology. I am growing cement
from the door down the driveway, spilling
into the street like welcome, or warning.

Identity Theft

I picked two strawberries in the garden
this morning before school.

My student was shot yesterday
sitting on her porch in Homewood.
Her brother had been murdered
last year. The trial for his killers
had just begun. Her name is China.
Unlike her brother, she will live.

A dog won't stop barking.
It's not my dog. Perhaps flowers
would be okay. Not a Get Well card.
Not a Glad They Got the Bullet Out card.

Between the birds and the bugs,
I lose a lot of berries, and I don't have many
to begin with in my tiny fenced-in yard.

The other students will know already.
They might know who did it too.
It works that way around here.

She'd told the shooters her name
when they asked. Identifying herself
as the victim. I don't think anyone
rots in hell. It's here where we rot.

I picked two strawberries in the garden
and immediately popped them in my mouth,
wiped the red juice from around my lips.

I wanted to pick more,
but that's all that were ripe.

Arguing about Guns, Again

We're gorging on Christmas cookies
and ravaging each other in our annual family battle.
My sister thinks the president must have a secret plan
(yeah, because nobody could deliberately sound that
    stupid),
my sister-in-law says, yeah, her sister was shot but those
    things
are always going to happen, my father says, just read
the papers, my cousin, a prison guard with an arsenal
    stashed
in his basement, cradles his infant daughter. He can't
    believe
we're going *there* again.

The moon, a bullet hole. The stars, specks of blood.
Snow, the stuffing of silence broken. The boat
is a soul's journey. The church is an egg.
Ambulance lights, the disco ball of tragedy.

My brother who, drunk, nearly shot a friend,
edges from the table—only I know that story—
he threw the gun in the river but now has another.
On the plate, leftovers crumble into a heap:
my sister-in-law's buckeyes, my mother's oatmeal
    gumdrops,
my sister's thumbprints, my children's sugar cookies.
So much sweetness on the one plate we share.

In the Shadow

of floodlights across the street
a pine tree spikes up three stories
near the roof of the rundown apartments
fading into night's dim shuffle.

On the street, a young couple *mother-*
fucks each other up and down the block,
the sound thundering into our dark rooms.

Some slam windows, others let the storm in,
staring down, hands firm on ledges.
Someone call the police, she screams,
before he kills me.

I do. She pulls away, then he's chasing her.
Once, I might have stepped out, intervened.
The thought of a gun freezes me in bare feet.

At least he hasn't hit her yet. I am a coward,
my heart, heavy stone, dropping. I flick off
the light and stand darkly watching them,
prickly like that pine, shivering like that pine.

Breath for My Mother, August

Night brakes squeal in the sizzling street.
The fan pants out stacked air.
Somebody shouts *love ain't no joke*.

    A bread wrapper festooned with stars
    you rustled open to slap six lunches
    together sandwich sandwich sandwich
    bread indented with your fingerprints
    napkin and apple and pennies for milk.

A siren and a moan
a siren and a moan
big mean dog chewing
a big mean bone.

    I'm not praying, just whispering
    cool air above the hot roofs
    sending it the old way
    no label or stamp.

Rancid street heat. Bodies half-heartedly
vicious over the scraps. I try to tune in
the voice believing in love.
A jeep's big speakers shakes the jitters
into concrete cracks.

You love me, still alive
with one lunch and six prayers—
fruit softening, rotting.

Who needs rain when we got
sweat when we got tears, salt on the lips
and a wish—salt on the lips
and a pistol raised? The moon swallows
bullets, or maybe that's a myth—

Hot there too, huh? Kick off
the sheets and turn the pillow,
no escaping the thumping bass
of the world's grudge.

Open your window wide
and listen for me.

Sweating Bullets at
"Sarah's Hair Spot"

Friday afternoon burning
tar sting and squint. Only May
but it's 90°. Hotter inside

where baby Brandon hangs
over a baby swing
that ain't swingin'.

Sarah's receptionist bailed
for the hospital—couldn't breathe,
she said. Might never come back.

Sarah cranks up the swing
takes me back into the cutting
room, WAMO funk, low on the radio—

bass-fuzz heart beats. Window shade
torn into cave-painted dinosaurs.

Is it one thing after another
or is it one long thing? Sarah asks.

I'm sweating bullets, I say.
Brandon's wailing. I'm liquifying
under the plastic sheet where my hair

lands softly. *I'm going to get air
in here,* Sarah assures me. *Once we get
off the ground.* The purple neon scissors

gone from the window, already repossessed.
Grand Opening, smudged with grit,
droops above the door.

WAMO thump, Brandon's treble wails.
Sarah picks him up and pats
his tiny sweating back, drops him

back in the swing. *There,* she says to me,
a summer haircut. Sweating bullets,
she repeats. A big woman.

It's just streaming off her like bad blood.
Her boyfriend, she says, is good with the baby.
Last week, another shooting across the street.

Sarah nods, and a drop hits the tile floor.
Drop.
Hits.

She'll be closed in a month, a sign
from the landlord taped to the door,
asking her to call.

Rubbled lot next door.
*Lucky I can bring him in with me—
don't know what I'd do.*

She wipes my hair off his face.
Getting gray already, little boy?
Baby swinging in the heat

silent at her touch. I pick a gray hair
off Brandon's black curls. *Ain't that
the truth,* Sarah says. Outside, somebody's

pounding a hammer, relentless as a wasp
at a crack in the cement. *Somebody
fixing up, not tearing down,*

I hope, Sarah says. She takes my money,
unlocks the door to let me out.
Cue the sirens.

Sunday Morning

A goldfinch bobs on a sunflower's head
picking out seeds behind Uncle Jimmy's Bar
where some guy got killed in a fight Friday night

before the Chinese restaurant next door
burned down. Investigations are taking place.
Details are sketched in chalk, erased by rain.
Graffiti codes indecipherable.

The sunflower, a volunteer from winter seeds,
gracefully allows itself to be picked apart,
gold blending into gold. Even the sparrows
are stunned by this yellow light.

Early Recess

A drive-by across from the kids' school.
A mother and her baby wailing on the stoop.

Boom boom. Lesson plan.
Duck and cover. Suspended animation.

Dream reels spinning a-tangle.
Where's my baby? Incubation period

missing at the end of the sentence.
Grammatical errors. Screamed

repetition of exclamation. Everybody
picking up their kids, taking them someplace

safe. Definitions of random. Pop quiz on Friday.
Guess who's packing and who's

buying. Not talking about lunch.
Not talking about the young hearts.

Outrage at the Laundromat

One stray dog trots in the open door
and on top of a basket of clean clothes
with its caked muddy paws, then under
the flat folding tables. An enormous
young woman stripped down to her bra
in the wild summer heat chases it out the door.
The rest of us, sweating, resigned to the spin
cycle, do not move a muscle. She's screaming
I'll kill that fucking dog as she storms back
in. Maybe somebody's smirk sets her
off. She turns on us. *Do I look like I got
any more fucking quarters, huh?* Her skin
a beautiful sheen of sweat. Okay.
We slap them down on the table
in front of her until she has enough
to start over.

Punching the Numbers

Two old men at the lottery/check-cashing
window grip aluminum canes and wait,
their lucky numbers memorized,
to be rattled off confidently in turn:
Straight. Boxed. Daily. Big Four.
Super Seven. The clerk will punch them
in just as quickly, the chain of her glasses
dangling, swaying, metronome
of dollar dreams, clutching the elusive.
One cane three-pronged, one rubber-tipped.

At the window, a young man speaks
a steady sweaty stream. The computer
says he's already cashed two checks today,
each at a different store. *What kinda check
you cashing?* The clerk steams bulletproof
between them.

Hey I done this before no problem
check's good I got credit last minute
something come up running late . . .

What *kinda check you cashing?*
The computer says . . .
His hands wobble and twist
on the slim counter. *Boy needs*

a cane himself, one man says.
The computer says . . .

You don't need it, she says.
Whatever it is, you don't
need it. The line sways back,
gives him space. *Go home.*
The clerk pushes a flat hand
against the smudged glass.
Her glasses and chain taut
against her chest. She calls security
on the tinny intercom. *You don't*
need . . . His skin sizzles
with fake love and high damage.
He raises both arms, *fuck you,*
all of you, the bad check flaps
in one hand as he backs toward
the door. As if he's just committed
a robbery. But already

one cane hooks the counter, the line
pulled tight again with the willingness
to give it up. 531, 470 8863, 25 36 17,
the chanting of the old monks
begins again.

Allergic to Bullets

His bright bones exposed to light.
People stared. Even small children,
reaching out to touch. Their parents
yanked them back. He quickly gave up
waving and smiling. Sharp metal
had pierced his ribs. He remembered
that much.

Did he know that angry man, cursing,
demanding? No, he did not. *What?*
was his last word. Many were upset
that he did not simply disappear
like the others, though certain birds
enjoyed his flesh while it lasted.

Here, the people said. *We have a stone
marker for you and everything.*
But he continued, rattling bones over
endless cement squares. The people
blamed the weakness of the flesh,
the flaw. Among them, the stranger
with the gun. A few shuffled their feet
and confessed their efforts to create
a vaccine had been unsuccessful.

He remembered when palms were open
in greeting, soft flesh exposed. If you've
come this far with me, you must have
seen him too. Or maybe heard
his footsteps echo. Or seen the dust
of his bones on the sidewalk.
Or heard the whistle through his ribs.
Or shielded your eyes
against the light.

The Shelter of My Father's Coat

Shots across the street again last night. My wife stood
at the window cursing tears. I took a sleeping
pill and floated through the swirling aftermath.
I dreamt of white sleep under the long protective
wings of my father's coat.

The paper never gets it right. Blotting out
blood-chill and bone-scream. But we read it
anyway. The world does not consist of
a vanity license plate and dancing
on the big screen at the ballgame.

This morning, the sliding glass door,
second floor, center apartment, is open.
11°, the paper says, blowing in. My children argue
over cereal. The world's microphone *testing,*
testing, but no pronouncement follows.

Just feedback. Shots across the street
again last night. Somebody not dead
but dying faster than the rest of us.
My wife is burnt toast and glower.
Was it random? Domestic? Drug-related?

She wants to know, to balance on the scale
of whether to move or not and where and what

we can afford. The fourth shooting in ten years.
Where does that balance on the world's
scale of violence? No sirens this morning,

just two police cars quietly parked. I slept,
but now coffee cuts the chemical haze,
lifts the day's cold mirage of peace.
If they ask me, I'll tell them the truth:
the snake crawls through every bullet hole.

The moon is ashamed. The river shuns us.
My father's coat stinks with the sweat
of forty years of being late. Those in the building
with jobs leave for work, heads down, as they must,

as if nothing happened. I swallow
one last bitter sip, and join them.